FAST FACTS

EXTREME SURVIVAL

JIM BRUSH

☀
SEA-TO-SEA
Mankato Collingwood London

This edition first published in 2012 by

Sea-to-Sea Publications
Distributed by Black Rabbit Books
P.O. Box 3263, Mankato, Minnesota 56002

Copyright © Sea-to-Sea Publications 2012

Printed in China

9 8 7 6 5 4 3 2

Published by arrangement with the Watts Publishing Group Ltd, London.

Library of Congress Cataloging-in-Publication Data

Brush, Jim.
  Extreme survival / by Jim Brush.
      p. cm. -- (Fast facts)
  Includes index.
  ISBN 978-1-59771-325-2 (library binding)
  1. Wilderness survival. 2. Survival skills. I. Title.
  GV200.5.B8 2012
  613.6'9--dc22
                                    2011001210

Series editor: Adrian Cole
Art director: Jonathan Hair
Design: Blue Paw Design
Picture research: Sophie Hartley
Consultants: Fiona M. Collins and Philippa Hunt, Roehampton University, UK

Acknowledgments:
Marina Alexdrova/istockphoto: front cover. Anthony Bannister//Corbis: 19b. blickwinkel/Alamy: 11 inset c, 28.
Bratan007/istockphoto: 8 inset b. Yvette Cardozo/Alamy: 24 inset. Ashley Cooper/Corbis: 29. Corbis: 22. Rob
Cousins/Alamy: 13. Angela Creekmur/Shutterstock: 15cl. Adam Hart-Davis/SPL: 16b. Neta Degany/istockphoto: 15l.
Mary Evans PL: 6. Robert Garvey/Corbis: 24-25. Geoffrey Grace/Alamy: 15t. Harwood Photography/Alamy: 8 main.
HiM/istockphoto: 23b. Hiob/istockphoto: 15cr. Rob Howard/Corbis: 26. IFC Films/Everett/Rex Features: 23t. Layne
Kennedy/Corbis: 16-17. Sandra Kourey/istockphoto: 9c. Clare Leimbach/Robert Harding/Corbis: 12. David Forster
Life/Alamy: 9cl. Albert Lozano/istockphoto: 8 inset t. Vasco Miokovic/istockphoto: 8 inset c. pomortzeff/istockphoto: 5
inset t, 25t. Chris Radburn/PA Archive/PAI: 7. Roger Ressmeyer/Corbis: 11 inset t. Jennifer Richards/istockphoto: 15c.
David Samuel Robbins/Corbis: 10-11. Joel W Rogers/Corbis: 5. Alexey Romanov/istockphoto: 9cr.
seaficus/istockphoto: 9crb. Alex Segre /Alamy: 5 inset b, 18. Sipa Press/Rex Features: 19t. David Spurdens/Corbis: 1,
16t, Benjamin Stansall/Alamy: 4. Alexey Stiop/Shutterstock: 20-21. Oliver Strewe/Corbis: 14. Ales Veluscek
/istockphoto: 9lt. Pat Wellenbach/AP/PAI: 20b. Stuart Westmorland/Corbis: 27. Anna Yu/istockphoto: 9b. Ariadne
van Zandbergen/Alamy: 15b. *Every attempt has been made to clear copyright. Should there be any inadvertent
omission please apply to the publisher for rectification.*

February 2011
RD/6000006415/001

*Every effort has been made by the Publishers to ensure that the web sites in this book contain
no inappropriate or offensive material. However, because of the nature of the Internet, it is
impossible to guarantee that the contents of these sites will not be altered. We strongly advise
that Internet access is supervised by a responsible adult.*

Contents

Words that are highlighted can be found in the glossary.

What Is Extreme Survival?

Extreme survival is about staying alive in the wildest places on Earth. People use special skills to survive.

These survival skills are also known as **bushcraft**. Bushcraft experts can build a shelter, create a fire, or find their way without a map. They can find food or hunt animals.

Bushcraft experts light fires with a spark and **tinder**.

Every **wilderness** has its own dangers. In the rain forest, it's easy to get lost. Deserts are baking hot. In the Arctic, it is freezing cold.

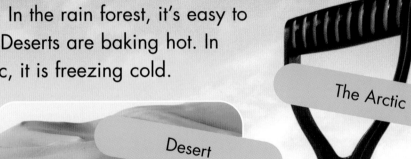
The Arctic

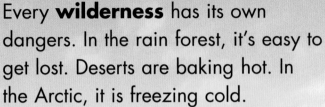
Desert

Rain Forest

? Which of the three places listed above are you most interested in learning more about, and why?

Be Prepared!

Explorers plan their adventures carefully. They think about where they are going and what they need to take. They follow the motto **of the** Scouts: **"Be prepared."**

FF Top Fact

Most explorers take only what they need. But in 1860, Robert Burke and William Wills (above center) set off across Australia with 8 tons of food, a bathtub, and a dining table. They left most of it in the desert.

Food and water are important for survival, but how much explorers need depends on where they are going. A journey across the desert needs lots of

? water. But polar explorers know they can boil snow on the way. What else will they need?

Will Gow and Henry Adams with their Antarctic expedition gear.

ONLINE//:

http://www.scouting.org/
Visit this web site to find out more about the Scouts and the wide range of activities they organize on land, at sea—and in the air.

Essential Gear

Imagine you're an explorer lost in the wilderness. Don't panic! A few pieces of equipment can help you stay alive.

A sharp knife does lots of jobs, from cutting wood to skinning an animal.

A **compass** helps to find a direction.

Flares attract attention in an emergency.

FF Top Fact

Canadian bushcraft expert Mors Kochanski once said: "The more you know, the less you carry."

A needle and thread repair torn clothing.

A **firesteel** or matches are a quick way to start a fire.

Fishhooks and line make catching fish a lot easier.

Candles provide light at night.

Fast Facts Survival Skill

A medical kit is vital. In 1844, explorer David Livingstone was attacked by a lion in Africa. Later, he was hit in the eye by a branch. Then he nearly went deaf due to fever.

ONLINE//:

http://www.raymears.com/Woodlore/Bushcraft_
Tips_And_Advice.cfm
Bushcraft tips on the web site of survival expert Ray Mears.

Lost!

Many explorers can find their way using only a compass. If they don't have one, there are other ways to find their direction.

If explorers don't have a map, they make one. They climb up a nearby hill to see farther. They use a compass to find north, then look for rivers and other features to use as markers.

FF Top Fact

To find north without a compass in Europe or North America, look for the Pole Star (circled). In Australia, the Southern Cross points to the south.

Fast Facts Survival Tip

Some plants can show the way. The compass plant (left) in North America has leaves that always point north–south. Or, in South Africa, north pole plants lean north.

Explorers also use the Sun to find their way. During the day, the Sun rises in the east and sets in the west. At night, stars can point the way. At sea, seaweed or seabirds can show that land is near.

ONLINE//:

www.us.orienteering.org
Web site of the U.S. Orienteering Federation, with links showing you how to use a compass, the gear you'll need, and an orienteering video.

Finding Water

A human can survive for three weeks without food, but only three days without water. Bushcraft experts always look for more water before they run out.

If there are no streams or pools, water can be found by digging in dry riverbeds or looking into rocky gaps. Also, plants such as bamboo, vines, and some roots hold water. Rainwater can be collected in a sheet or container.

Drinking rainwater from a cut vine in the rain forest.

Experts save water by staying in the shade to avoid sweating. They also only talk when they need to. Drinking urine or salty seawater are not good ideas.

ONLINE//:

www.cultureandrecreation.gov.au/articles/indigenous/trackers   This site by the Australian government looks at the remarkable tracking skills of the Aboriginal peoples of Australia.

Hunting and Fishing

Bushcraft experts know what wild plants can be eaten. They can also track and hunt animals. Food found in the wild is sometimes called bushfood.

Australian honey ants are rich in **nutrients** and water.

All sorts of plants can provide food— from stewed seaweed and cups of pine-needle tea to bamboo shoots. But some plants are **poisonous**, so only experts should find bushfood.

Hunters learn where an animal sleeps and eats. They catch small animals such as lizards and rabbits in simple traps, like this (right).

 Paw prints and droppings show what animals are nearby. Try to figure out what made these four tracks:

A B C D

Tribesmen in parts of Africa learn how to hunt as they grow up.

ONLINE//:

www.bear-tracker.com
If you want to try tracking down some animals in North America, this site is a great place to start. It includes the tracks shown above.

In the wild, building a fire provides heat and cooks food. A shelter offers protection from the Sun, wind and rain—and even wild animals.

Bushcraft experts can start a fire by creating sparks to set dry grass alight. They hit **flint** with a steel knife, use a firesteel, or use a bow and drill (left). They add dry twigs and leaves, called tinder, to get the fire going. Then they put larger sticks on top.

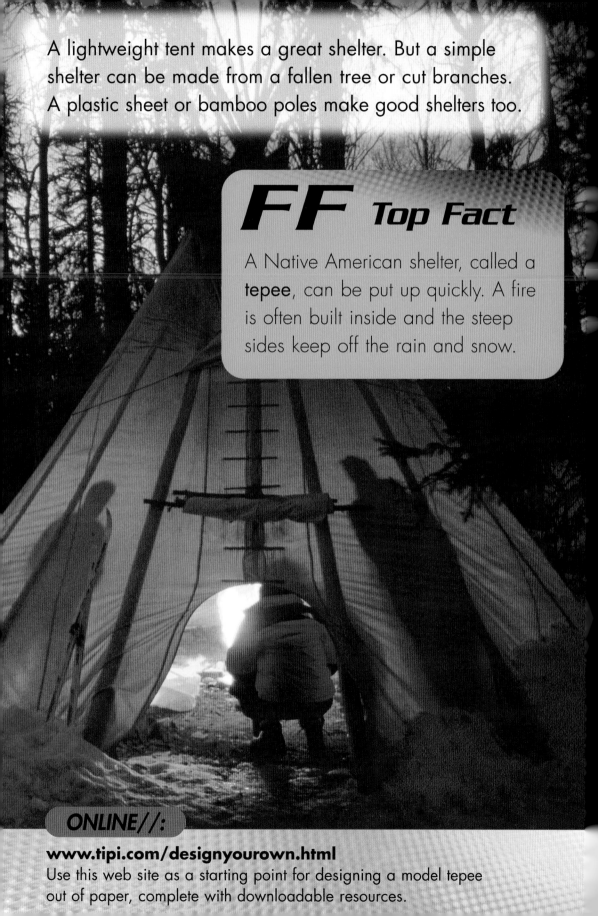

A lightweight tent makes a great shelter. But a simple shelter can be made from a fallen tree or cut branches. A plastic sheet or bamboo poles make good shelters too.

FF Top Fact

A Native American shelter, called a **tepee**, can be put up quickly. A fire is often built inside and the steep sides keep off the rain and snow.

ONLINE//:

www.tipi.com/designyourown.html
Use this web site as a starting point for designing a model tepee out of paper, complete with downloadable resources.

Rain Forests

In the rain forest, it's hot and humid. Trekking through the forest is hard work. Jaguars, crocodiles, and snakes can kill. Creepy crawlies give a painful bite.

Trekking in the Amazon rain forest in South America.

FF Top Fact

In 1971, teenager Juliane Koepcke survived a plane crash in the Amazon rain forest. The other 92 passengers died. She followed rivers downhill and walked out of the jungle 10 days later, with a torn miniskirt and one sandal.

Rain forest explorers wear boots and special wraps around the bottom of their pants. This stops **leeches** from getting on their skin (above). At night, they sleep under nets to protect against mosquitoes. A mosquito bite can give people a deadly disease called **malaria**.

ONLINE//:

http://www.exploratorium.edu/frogs/rainforest/
index.html   Audio clips of frogs in the rain forest—close
your eyes and imagine what it's like to be lost.

Lost at Sea

The ocean is a tough place to stay alive. Storms cause high waves and the hot Sun can quickly burn skin and cause dehydration.

In 1982, Steve Callahan (below) was crossing the Atlantic Ocean. His boat sank in a storm. For the next 76 days, he survived on a tiny raft.

Steve made a spear to catch fish and seabirds. He fought off sharks that attacked his raft. When Steve's raft sprang a leak, he kept it afloat. He drifted almost 1,900 miles (3,000 km) before he was spotted by a fishing boat. Later, he wrote a book: *Adrift—Seventy-six Days Lost at Sea*.

Fast Facts Survival Skill

Steve used a solar still. This uses the heat of the Sun to turn salty seawater into drinking water.

Solar still

1. Dome lets in sunlight and traps heat.

2. Heat from the Sun's rays evaporates seawater.

3. Evaporated seawater condenses (cools and becomes water) and flows into the rim.

4. Distilled water (water separated from sea salt) collects in a container.

ONLINE//:

www.wilderness-survival.net
A great source of survival stories both at sea and on land, as well as useful information on equipment and planning.

Mountains

On a mountain there is very little food or shelter. Plane crash survivors and lost mountaineers need both skill and luck.

Crash survivors can find shelter among rocks or in the plane wreckage. They can wrap themselves in blankets to keep warm. For most people, it is safer to wait until rescue comes.

Mountaineers who get lost can use ropes and other equipment to climb down. They watch out for falling rocks and **avalanches**.

FF Top Fact

In 1985, Joe Simpson broke his leg climbing in Peru. He crawled down to safety. Later, he wrote a book called *Touching the Void*, which was made into a movie (left).

Fast Facts Survival Skill

Grizzly bears live in mountain areas of the U.S. and Canada. Most will see you as a tasty snack. What should you do if you are attacked?

ONLINE//:

www.kids.nationalgeographic.com/Animals/CreatureFeature/Brown-bear   There's a whole range of facts, photos, and video clips on brown bears at this site.

Deserts

Deserts are beautiful but deadly places. In a hot desert, a person without the right clothes, water, and shade in the morning could be dead by evening.

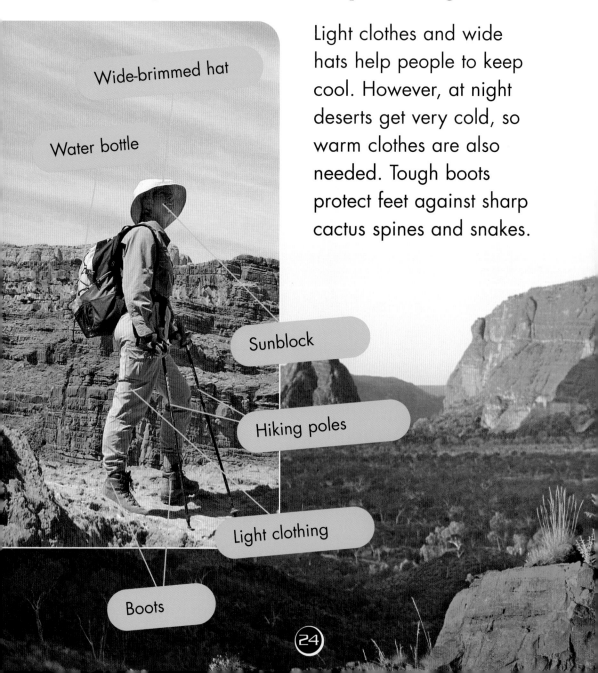

Wide-brimmed hat

Water bottle

Sunblock

Hiking poles

Light clothing

Boots

Light clothes and wide hats help people to keep cool. However, at night deserts get very cold, so warm clothes are also needed. Tough boots protect feet against sharp cactus spines and snakes.

It is hard to cross a desert. Huge sand dunes block the way and cars can get stuck in the soft sand. Camels are the perfect desert transportation. Why do you think the camel is called the "ship of the desert"?

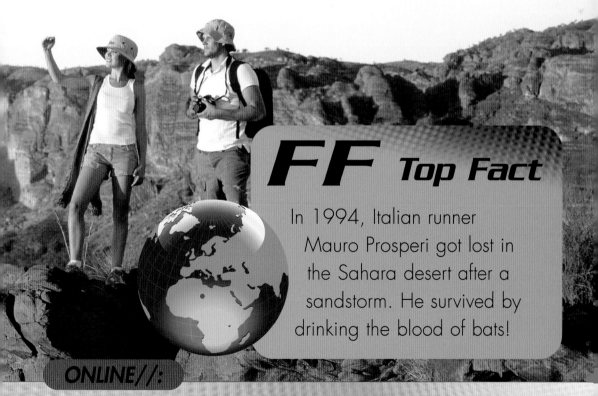

FF Top Fact

In 1994, Italian runner Mauro Prosperi got lost in the Sahara desert after a sandstorm. He survived by drinking the blood of bats!

ONLINE//:

www.desertusa.com/mag99/mar/stories/desertsur.html
Check out this web site for great information on desert survival, desert animals, a survival kit, and desert-linked videos.

At the Poles

At the poles, it's incredibly cold and very windy. The ground is covered in a thick layer of ice. Snowstorms, called blizzards, can bury things deep in snow.

This Inuit man is wearing a hooded jacket called a parka.

To survive at the poles, it is important to stay warm and dry. If someone gets too cold, they can easily die. Arctic peoples, such as the Inuit, wear thick jackets and boots. Many explorers also wear sun goggles, because looking at the bright snow can make people blind.

An igloo built from ice provides shelter from freezing winds. There are no edible plants in these freezing conditions, so people hunt seals or penguins for food. Near the North Pole, explorers stay on the lookout for fierce polar bears.

Fast Facts Survival Skill

Beware of deep cracks in the ice, called crevasses. In 1903, polar explorer Robert Scott fell down one, but managed to climb out.

Igloos have a single entrance to stop heat from escaping.

ONLINE//:

www.pbs.org/wnet/nature/fun/arctic_flash.html
Learn how the Inuit people use Arctic animals to help them survive on the ice, plus play the penguin Antarctic survival game.

Rescue

Survivors must let others know where they are if they are to be rescued.

Here are the best ways to let a rescue boat or helicopter know where you are:

- Light a fire in a high place.
- Use a mirror or piece of glass to reflect sunlight.
- Switch a flashlight on and off.

FF Top Fact

Mountain rescue teams often use dogs to find survivors. They follow **scent** carried on the air, even if people have been buried under an avalanche.

Helicopters are often used to conduct rescues. If a helicopter can't land, it can hover while survivors are winched up into it.

Fast Facts Survival Skill

Many explorers and sailors carry flares with them in case of an emergency. Hand flares (above) can be waved. Flare guns fire bright flares high into the sky.

ONLINE//:

www.mra.org/drupal2/   Find out more about The Mountain Rescue Association (MRA), established in 1959 in Oregon—the oldest Search and Rescue association in the U.S.

Answers

These are suggested answers to questions in this book. You may find that you have other answers. Talk about them with your friends. They may have other answers, too.

Page 5: The answer to this question will depend on your own opinion.

Page 7: Polar explorers can only take what they can carry and drag on sleds. Important equipment includes very warm clothing, sun goggles, gloves, boots, skis, sleds, ice picks, a snow shovel, rope, a gas stove and a pot, a tent, food, maps, and a **GPS** device.

Page 15: A=bear, B=deer, C=wolf, D=rabbit. Don't forget, some wild animals such as bears or wolves might be following you!

Page 23: If you meet a bear, put your hands in the air to look bigger, then back away. If you have a backpack, throw it at the bear. It might give you time to escape—but don't run because the bear will chase you.

Pages 25: Camels are called "ships of the desert" because they provide the most reliable way of traveling in tough desert conditions. They don't have to drink often, can travel long distances, and have wide, padded feet that don't sink into the sand.

Glossary

Aborigines—the first people who lived in Australia and Tasmania.

Avalanches—a large amount of snow that slides down a mountain.

Bushcraft—the skills needed to survive in the wild, such as finding food and making tools.

Compass—a device used for finding your way. Compass needles always point north.

Dehydration—when the body loses too much water, for example, from sweating.

Firesteel—a rod made of mixed metals that produces sparks when scraped with steel. Also called a fire striker or a fire starter.

Flares—devices for making very bright light to attract help.

Flint—a hard stone struck with a piece of steel to create a spark—perfect for lighting fires.

GPS—global positioning system, a satellite system that allows people to find their position anywhere on Earth.

Leeches—blood-sucking creatures that look like slugs.

Malaria—a disease spread by the bite of a mosquito.

Motto—a word or phrase that sums up the ideals of a group.

Nutrients—the chemicals humans, animals, and plants need to grow and stay alive.

Poisonous—something that contains poison and is dangerous to eat.

Scent—smell left behind by a person or animal that allows them to be tracked.

Scout—a person who goes ahead to explore, find a route, or look out for danger. Also, a member of the Boy Scouts Association.

Tepee—a Native American tent made of bison skin stretched over a frame of wooden poles (and shaped like a cone). Also called a tipi.

Tinder—dry wood shavings, or other material used to start a fire.

Wilderness—a wild place with no or very few people.

Index